The Compound Interest Millionaire:

Hack Your Savings to Create a Constant Stream of Passive Income

By

Joe Correa

Copyright

Acknowledgements

This book could not have been written without the support and motivation of my family. May all the people in the world that want a better financial future for themselves and their family, find this to be a useful and practical tool to reach that objective.

The Compound Interest Millionaire:

Hack Your Savings to Create a Constant Stream of Passive Income

By

Joe Correa

About the author

For many years I have helped people to finance a home or to lower their payments. I have worked for different banks, lenders, and an investment advisory firm. I started as a college math professor at Miami-Dade Community College teaching all subjects I was asked to teach at age 23, which was kind of awkward for many of my students since most were around my age or older but my ability to teach others and to master math helped me make difficult subjects become easy to understand. That's why my classes became larger and larger. I was approached by Union Planters Bank which is now Regions Bank to work for them as a Financial Sales Representative at one of their branches. This was an important learning stage for me that allowed me to learn about the importance helping others. On a daily basis, I complete home equity lines of credit and home equity loans, and many other tasks. I especially enjoyed closing home equity loans and wanted to learn more so I got my mortgage license and went to work for a mortgage company. A year later I started my own mortgage business and soon transitioned to a correspondent lender. I was able to help hundreds of people to buy a home, refinance to lower payments, and to improve their financial lives. When the economy slowed down and banks stopped lending I decided to focus on helping investors by becoming an investment advisor. I got my series 67 license and started my own investment advisory business. Most investors had lost trust in the economy and did not want to reinvest so I decided to help by educating them through my books.

Introduction

The compound interest millionaire: Hack your savings to create a constant stream of passive income

By Joe Correa

The compound interest millionaire is a person that gets paid interest every month instead of paying interest to a bank or someone else. This person has time to enjoy the good things in life instead of working a 9 to 5 job they don't like. The compound interest millionaire has no special abilities or high IQ. The person simply learned the secret of compound interest and put it to good use.

Would you believe me if I told you any one could become a compound interest millionaire? All you need is: a monthly income to be able to save every month, compound interest to make those savings grow, and knowledge of how to reorganize you're finances. This book will give you that knowledge and show you every step of the way.

What is compound interest? Compound interest is the interest you receive on money you have deposited in a bank account that can compound on a monthly basis. It's also known as "interest on interest". Most banks offer savings accounts that compound interest monthly which is one of the best ways to accumulate money over time.

Imagine if you could receive an additional income every month in the form of interest paid by the bank.

How is this possible?

Let's say after you deduct all expenses from your current income (salary or business profits) you are able to save $2,000 every month and you deposit this amount into an interest earning savings account that earns a 1% annual percentage yield (APY) which would be your annual rate of return when taking into account the amazing effect of compound interest. After 30 years, you would have $839,256.

If you were able to increase the amount you save per month to $2,500, you would have $1,049,071 after 30 years. By increasing your saving capacity every month by only $500, you were able to save a total of $1,049,071.

This is how your money would compound over 30 years when you save $2,500 every month and earn an interest rate of 1%. You would earn over $800 every month simply from interest. If you are receiving a higher interest rate, you would be able to save even more and increase your passive income.

This is an incredible amount of money you could retire on by simply making monthly deposits of $2,500 and earning a 1% interest that compounds monthly in your savings account. It sounds too good to be true but that's the power of compound interest.

This book will teach you how to become a compound interest millionaire by following simple steps that will maximize the compounding effect you can have on your financial life.

You can be wealthy without having to do anything special or be a genius. If you're able to become wealthy doing something else, do it by all means, but this is one way to do it following a simple process that requires very little time and effort.

The best thing about compound interest is that you can receive this form of income every month without having to do anything at all after you have deposited your monthly savings into your interest earning savings account that compounds monthly.

Why isn't everyone doing this?

Some people never do the numbers so they don't know what it all adds up to in the end. Other people are skeptical when it comes to money. Some just want to become wealthy overnight but that's not how long-lasting money is made. As they say "easy come, easy go". How many times have you heard of the signer, actor, or even athlete that becomes wealthy overnight and then loses it all in a few years? Learning to manage money can be very simple and rewarding.

Stop paying interest and get started receiving interest income every month!

What are you waiting for? Get to it.

Contents

Chapter 1

The Compound Interest Millionaire

"Compound interest is the eighth wonder of the world."

Albert Einstein

The compound interest millionaire is a person who does not rely on job income any more. This person follows a specific financial plan every day and sticks to it. The compound millionaire has interest earning interest. This person has interest compounding frequently, the shorter the time frame, the more powerful the effect. These interest payments the compound interest millionaire receives continually grow over time. This person has more time to enjoy life and time with family.

Anyone can become a compound interest millionaire if you make the decision to change your life and reverse the financial tables. Instead of paying interest every month, start receiving interest payments. Over time the interest income in your account will create a powerful effect on your overall finances and your life in general. Interest can be consistent and safe income that you can receive on a monthly basis.

Why isn't everyone a compound interest millionaire?

First, they must think it's possible so that they have the right frame of mind. Second, sacrifices need to be made at the beginning and restructuring debt and expenses becomes a priority. Third, the habit of saving every month a specific amount would need to be automatic. Fourth, they would need to consistent with the process every month. These four things are why most people are not compound interest millionaires.

If I do these four things, will I become a compound interest millionaire?

Yes, there are specific details you have to take into account but in general these four things will allow you to become a compound interest millionaire:

1. Lower or eliminate most of your expenses
2. Save a specific amount of money every month
3. Put that money in an interest earning savings account that compounds monthly and not withdraw it.
4. Increase your income by starting your own business so that you can save more.

How you do these four things will be the main difference since some people save very little while others have too many expenses.

Is the interest received every month the most important thing when trying to become a compound interest millionaire?

Yes, the interest received each month is important and it does help to accelerate the process but the general habit of saving is what really makes the biggest difference over time. The most important thing to do is consistently make monthly deposits into your interest earning savings account so it can compound monthly.

What's the fastest way to increase my income in order to save more?

The fastest way to earn more is by spending less. This includes, eliminating debt payments and unnecessary expenses and other monthly fees. For example, if you got rid of $1,000 in monthly expenses it could be the equivalent of receiving $1,500 more in income if you're an employee and have taxes taken from your check every month and other deductions. Eliminating $1,000 in payments and expenses every month and depositing them into a 1% interest earning savings account would become just over $419,628 when compounded monthly over 30 years.

How can something this simple be so profitable?

Compound interest is powerful and effective. People that become good at spending make it a habit of spending and people that are good at saving make it a habit of saving. The habit of saving has greatly diminished in our society. Using credit cards instead of debit cards is common and has become a serious problem in most households. Following the crowd is not the solution. The solution comes from using age old methods that worked in the past and work even better now. Saving works and increasing interest income by using compound interest gives savings a big boost over time.

When should I start using compound interest?

As soon as possible. The sooner you start, the faster your savings will grow which will allow you to receive higher interest payments, which in turn will accelerate the savings process. That's why it's so important to open an interest earning savings account today (that compounds monthly) and begin to make consistent deposits into the account so that interest starts to accrue right away. Start young and don't stop making deposits. If you are older, simply focus on making larger deposits into your interest earning savings account. Age can become irrelevant if other factors weigh more heavily like: how much you save per month, what interest rate you are getting paid, not making withdrawals from your savings account, keeping your taxable income low (ask your accountant about this), etc.

What does it mean to have interest compound monthly?

When interest is compounded monthly, you receive monthly interest payments on the money you originally deposited and then receive interest on that interest and the original money you had deposited. That's why compound interest is commonly referred to as "interest on interest".

When interest is compounded yearly, you will get paid interest on an annual basis on the cash deposited. Monthly payments are always better than annual interest payments.

When interest is compounded daily, you will get paid interest on a daily basis so you will be able to earn interest on interest on a daily basis. Daily compounded interest is better than monthly or annually compounded interest as you will receive more money at the end of your savings plan. There are even some banks that offer daily interest compounding savings accounts. Research online to see who they are and what they offer.

What is the difference between annual percentage rate and annual percentage yield?

There is a very big difference between these two. In one you are paying interest and on the other one you are receiving interest payments.

An annual percentage rate or APR, as it is commonly known, is the annual rate of interest <u>you pay</u> on borrowed funds. It does not take into account compounded interest but if you make the minimum payment on a credit card you will end up carrying interest over to the following month which then does become compounded interest because you will start paying interest on interest owed. This is the rate you normally pay when you get most types of loans. Common examples of loans are: home loans, car loans, credit cards, personal loans, student loans, etc.

An annual percentage yield or APY, as it is also known, is the effective annual rate of return <u>you are paid</u> when you are taking into account the amazing effect of compound interest. This is the rate you are quoted when you deposit money in a savings account or most interest earning bank accounts that compound interest.

There is a big difference in paying interest on loans (APR) versus getting paid interest on savings (APY), especially when the second can compound on a monthly basis to your favor. Not knowing the difference can be a problem but not to worry, we will go over what steps you can take to correct this.

Your goal is to shift from paying an APR (on a loan) to getting paid an APY (on savings). That's why paying off debts and saving more money is so important to your future. It's the difference between being poor and in debt or wealthy and prospering.

APR = bad

APY = good

It's as simple as that!

Review your current situation and see in what category you're in. Are in the APR category or in the APY category? Do you owe a lot of money or have money saved?

How often does interest compound?

Interest can compound daily (365 times a year), monthly (12 times a year), quarterly (4 times a year), Semi-annually (2 times a year), or annually (1 time a year). Some banks offer daily compounding interest which would benefit you even more than compounding interest on an annual basis. Most banks offer a monthly compounding interest rate, which means you are getting paid interest on a monthly basis so that interest can compound again and again every month. This is called getting paid "interest on interest".

Is it better to get paid interest on a daily basis or annual basis?

The sooner you get paid, the better. When you go to your bank ask them if they're savings account pays interest on a monthly or daily basis. If they say it's paid on a semi-annual or annual basis, go to another bank. If it's paid daily or monthly that is fine. Some online banks offer the best rates and even offer daily compounding interest savings accounts. Make sure they are federally insured deposits (FDIC insured). Also, compare interest rates on savings accounts as some banks pay almost nothing in interest while others pay a significant amount. If one bank is popular or you have friends there but they pay a low interest rate, go to another bank that pays more. Make compound interest one of your best friends from now on. Remember, the sooner interest compounds, the faster your savings will grow. Monthly interest compounding savings accounts are the most common form of payment frequency offered by banks.

Should I open a children's savings account for my kids?

This is one of the best things you can do for your children, especially if you start making deposits into that account when they are young. The younger, the better. Compounding interest for more years can only benefit you.

Even if you make very small deposits into your kid's accounts every month, the interest will compound and when the time comes they will have enough saved to buy a house, start a business, go to college, or to continue compounding interest. Again, make sure to shop at different banks for the best rates as you will find some kid's savings accounts can offer a very high interest rate.

Are automatic bank transfers a good or bad idea?

I am often amazed to see how many people accept to have their monthly bills withdrawn from their bank accounts automatically every month, but physically make deposits into their savings account. When considering whether or not to have money transferred from your bank account to pay bills or to your savings account, make sure you give your savings account transfers priority and then give your bills second priority. It's been a money management rule for many years, "always pay yourself first". If you don't find a way to pay yourself first, you will end up with nothing left over to deposit into your savings account once you pay all your debts and expenses.

Remember APY has priority over APR. You should be getting paid interest first and foremost and in order to do this, you need to save first.

What is more valuable time or money?

Both are important but time is more valuable because you can run out of time, no one is printing more time, and you can't buy more time no matter how much money you have. Interest income is considered a form a passive income because you don't have to work to earn this income. By not having to work for that income, you free up time. This free time can be used to do and enjoy other things now that you don't have to work for that money. Consider how valuable this can be.

CHAPTER SUMMARY

Understanding compounded interest can be tricky at the beginning but once you start earning it, you will see what it means to receive interest on interest every month. It does not matter if you can make small deposits or large deposits. All that matters is that you start and stick with it. Make sure you research to make sure your interest earning savings account compounds interest on a monthly basis or even daily. Never make interest payments, always plan on receiving interest payments by using your savings account to compound interest and pay you every month. Consider opening a kid's savings account if you have children and want to get them started soon.

Chapter 2

Forms of Passive Income and Their Degree of Risk

"We draw compound interest on the whole capital of knowledge and virtue which has been accumulated since the dawning of time."

Arthur Conan Doyle

Earning passive income should be your ultimate goal. Passive income is income you receive where you work or not. Most people work hard to save and accumulate things but if those things can't generate passive income, then you will have to continue working to generate income. Creating passive income is easier said than done but with some effort and some planning you can get started on the right track. There are simple but effective forms of passive income that you can start receiving but it's important to understand what they are and what they require. Let's go over some of the most common forms of passive income that are available to people who are looking to create a new stream of passive income.

1. INTEREST INCOME FROM A SAVINGS ACCOUNT

When you have a savings account, your money is available immediately and most of the time you don't have to maintain a minimum deposit.

If the interest earned is compounded monthly, you are on the right track and should be the only way you should make a deposit. Always take advantage of higher interest rates being offered. Some online banks have the best rates so that might be something you want to research to find out what they offer. Some banks require minimum deposit amounts while others don't have minimums. Some banks require that you have a direct deposit every month made into your account while others don't. Look for a savings account that has a high interest rate, compounds interest monthly, and has few requirements and restrictions. This will keep things simple and will help you achieve your goal of creating passive income. You should see an interest payment deposited into your savings account every month. You did little or no work for that money and that's the magic of passive income. If you have money laying around in a non-interest accruing checking account or other place, you lose out on passive income you could have on a monthly basis. Most savings account deposits are FDIC insured but always make sure this applies to your bank as well.

2. INTEREST INCOME FROM A CERTIFICATE OF DEPOSIT

On certificates of deposit, your money is not available until the term of the certificate ends unless you pay fees or other bank imposed expenses. Make sure your deposits are FDIC insured. CD's as they are often called, don't compound interest monthly since you are paid the interest due when the certificate expires which could be in 3 months, 4 months, 6 months, 1 year, 2 years, 3 years, or even 5 years. It's still passive income since you don't have to work for that money but you have to wait for the certificate to expire to receive your interest plus original deposit. Always make sure you go to the bank when the certificate of deposit expires as some banks automatically renew your certificate after some time has passed. Check with your bank representative as each bank offers different products.

3. INTEREST INCOME FROM A MONEY MARKET ACCOUNT

In money market accounts your funds are available immediately but will often require that the account be opened and maintained with a specific minimum amount to prevent fees and charges. Also, most money market accounts have restrictions as to how many deposits and withdrawals are made each month. The beneficial aspect of money market accounts is that the interest rate is normally higher than a savings account or certificate of deposit which means you will receive higher interest payments. When you have higher interest payments your passive income is higher as well and your capacity to compound interest monthly will be faster. Most money market accounts are FDIC insured but always check with your bank or research online to review all the account requirements. Also, make sure the interest is compounded on a monthly or even daily basis which is commonly how interest is compounded on these accounts.

4. INTEREST FROM AN ANNUITY

Interest rates are usually higher but funds are not available without a penalty until a specific age and you must be a specific age to start as well. Risk of non-repayment is higher than the last three options. This financial product is not FDIC insured so it has a higher degree of risk. Check with your financial planner or bank representative for more details.

5. REAL ESTATE RENTAL INCOME

Rental income from real estate is a great way to receive passive income. This form of passive income does require that you maintain the property you are renting in good state for your tenants. Things means, if the refrigerator stops working in one of your rental properties, you must fix it or call someone to go and fix it and pay them for their services. You also have additional expenses to cover like:

insurance, taxes, lawn mowing, sometimes water and electricity (if they are not paid by the tenant). When you rent real estate you are considered the landlord. In a sense, the income you receive on a monthly basis in the form of rent payments, can be compounded monthly if you reinvested the cash into another rental property every month but that would require that you receive substantial amounts of rental income to buy more real estate. After all expenses, the income that is left over from the rental payment is your passive income. This can be a great form of passive income if you are able to eliminate most of the expenses and don't have to fix things constantly. Some people buy a rental property and rent it until the mortgage is paid off and then own it free of mortgage payments. At that point, they start receiving positive cash flow from their rental, which basically means they are making money after all expenses are paid.

Never buy a rental property where you have negative cash flow, which means a property where you have more expenses than income and you end up taking money out of your pocket to cover for the negative difference in cash flow.

As an added benefit to owning rental properties, your real estate properties can go up in value over time which will allow you to have more options. Having more equity, which is the difference between what you owe on your mortgage and what the property is actually worth, can benefit you when applying for a loan on another rental property. It can also benefit you when you decide to sell the rental property and make a profit on the sale.

Purchasing rental properties to generate rental income will require a more hands-on approach than the last four passive income options mentioned before but can become another form of passive income for you over time.

6. CASH DIVIDEND INCOME FROM STOCKS

When you purchase stock from a company you could receive dividend payments in the form of cash if the company offers that benefit when you own shares in the company. Some dividend payments are made monthly, some quarterly, and some annually. The price of the stock you purchase can go up or down and this will affect the dividend payment you receive and can be the main risk for this type of passive income. For people that receive company stock as a form of payment besides their salary, this can be a major benefit. For people who purchase stock just to receive dividend payments, make sure to consult with a financial planner or an investment advisor as owning stocks can have significant risk or reward. Stocks are not FDIC insured.

7. INCOME FROM BUSINESS PROFITS

Owning a business or franchise can be very beneficial. Owning a business can mean several things. A business can provide you with consistent passive income, tax benefits, and flexibility. It can also mean you could be working longer hours and barely making enough income to cover expenses. Owning a business can mean having a high risk/reward result. This means, you can either be very successful or very unsuccessful.

The big difference between this type of passive income and the others mentioned before, is that it can be almost entirely up to you how successful you are. You might have to put in long hours for the first few years to help your company grow and start seeing consistent passive income if your business has been structured correctly.

Many people start businesses because of the tax benefits it offers. For example, when you receive a salary, taxes are deducted before you are paid and then you use that money to pay for your expenses. When you have your own business, you deduct expenses first and then pay taxes on that money. Everybody's situation is different so make sure to consult with your accountant before starting your own business.

SUMMARY

My favorite form of passive income is interest income from savings accounts or money market accounts because they offer the most flexibility and liquidity (my money is available any time). But the most important reason why they are a great option is because interest compounds on a monthly basis which is how you will accumulate money faster over time in a consistent and reliable manner. This will allow you to have more free time to do other things. You can decide what you prefer to do with your money just make sure to consult with your financial planner or accountant to make sure it's right for.

CHAPTER SUMMARY

There are many types of passive income and each one has its own degree of risk. You have to choose how much risk you take but it's important to know that you don't have to take risks to receive passive income. Interest income from savings accounts is a very simple and easy way to create passive income on a monthly basis. Make sure to consider all of your options and decide what best suites you and the lifestyle you want to have in the future. Having passive income is a great way to generate income, especially when it's on a monthly basis.

Chapter 3

Hacking Your Credit Card Debt to Create Passive Income

"An investment in knowledge pays the best interest."

Benjamin Franklin

If your credit card payment each month is $300 and you owe $17,000 this means you have $300 that could be used to save and create interest income. If you have a 15% interest rate on your credit card, you would need to find an investment that makes at least 15% in order to receive the same $300 in income. If you had $17,000 on hand that you could use to pay off your credit card debt, it would be a good decision to pay it off since most investments that pay you 15% will require some form of risk on your part but paying off your credit card has no risk as long as you have additional savings for your future expenses. The same $300 you wouldn't have to pay every month to your credit card company would now go towards your interest earning savings account. From now on you will receive passive income every month. We are replacing interest payments with interest income. We are switching APR for APY so we will see growth, not debt over the years. Let's see how much we could accumulate over 30 years using a compound interest calculator with an interest rate of 1% compounded monthly.

THE NUMBERS BEHIND IT ALL:

Current financial situation (CFS):

Credit card debt: $17,000

Monthly credit card payments: $300

Other expenses: $950

Savings account: $25,000

Monthly income: $4,000

Income minus credit card payment and other expenses will give you how much you can save every month.

$4,000 - $300 - $950 = $2,750

This is what you have available to start earning compound interest on: $2,750

If you save $2,750 every month and deposit this amount into an interest earning savings account that compounds monthly you will have a total of $1,187,720 after 30 years (assuming you start with an initial deposit of $25,000 which is being used in this example).

Let review how the interest compound every year:

Year 1: $58,403

Year 2: $92,141

Year 3: $126,219

Year 4: $160,638

Year 5: $195,404

Year 6: $230,518

Year 7: $265,986

Year 8: $301,810

Year 9: $337,993

Year 10: $374,540

Year 11: $411,455

Year 12: $448,740

Year 30: $1,187,720

We skipped year 13 – 29 to simplify the example but the key is to notice the gradual growth when using compound interest.

Improved financial situation (IFS):

You are now going to pay off your credit card debt using your savings. You should now have this income available every month:

$4,000 - $950 = $3,050

This is what you have available to start earning compound interest on: $3,050

If you save $3,050 every month and deposit this amount into an interest earning savings account that compounds monthly you will have a total of $1,290,664 after 30 years (assuming you start with an initial deposit of $8,000 in savings which is being used in this example after paying off your credit card debt).

Let review how the interest compound every year:

Year 1: $44,849

Year 2: $82,067

Year 3: $119,660

Year 4: $157,630

Year 5: $195,982

Year 6: $234,719

Year 7: $273,845

Year 8: $313,365

Year 9: $353,281

Year 10: $393,598

Year 11: $434,320

Year 12: $475,452

Year 30: $1,290,664

We skipped years 13 – 29 to simplify the example but the key is to notice the gradual growth when using compound interest.

The difference between paying off your credit card or not after 30 years was $102,944. You made $102,944 more by paying off $17,000 in credit card debt. This was a 16.5% return on your credit card pay off investment. This was a smart decision.

$17,000/$102,944 = 16.5%

Let's compare how much you could save over 30 years by using different credit card payment amounts:

If you make $250 in credit card payments every month you could save a total of $104,907 in 30 years by paying your debt off and depositing the same amount in an interest earning savings account that compounds interest on a monthly basis that pays an interest rate of 1%.

If you make $450 in credit card payments every month you could save a total of $188,833 in 30 years by paying the debt off and depositing the same amount in an interest earning savings account that compounds interest on a monthly basis that pays an interest rate of 1%.

If you make $750 in credit card payments every month you could save a total of $314,721 in 30 years by paying off your debts and depositing the same amount in an interest earning savings account that compounds interest on a monthly basis that pays an interest rate of 1%.

If you make $1,500 in credit card payments every month you could save a total of $629,442 in 30 years by paying off your debts and depositing the same amount in an interest earning savings account that compounds interest on a monthly basis that pays an interest rate of 1%.

CREDIT CARD PAY OFF PLAN

Having a credit card pay off plan is essential. Here are some things you can do to pay off your credit card debt sooner:

1. Call the bank and ask them to lower your interest rate.
2. Call the bank and negotiate a lower pay off amount. This works well when you offer to pay it off in full or when you have had late payments.
3. Increase your credit score to obtain a low interest credit card and transfer the high interest credit card debt to the low interest card.
4. Make additional principal payments to your lower balance credit cards and pay them off.
5. Pay off credit cards that require the highest monthly payment to free up cash.
6. Refinance your home and consolidate debt by including your credit cards in your mortgage and having only one payment at a low and fixed interest rate.
7. Use your savings to pay off all your credit card debt. Just make sure you have enough money saved for emergencies. In general, always have 6 - 12 months of total home payments in savings in case you lose your job or you lose your current source of income. Being prepared is better than getting caught off guard and having to resort to additional debt instead of getting out of debt.

CHAPTER SUMMARY

Paying interest on credit cards is a big problem many people have around the world. The key is to eliminate this problem by paying off all your debts and doing whatever is necessary to start saving so you can earn passive income in the form of interest income. Remember, paying interest is bad and earning interest is good. Earning compound interest is the real goal when trying to obtain true financial stability and growth. Debt is never the solution so make a plan and stick to it.

Chapter 4

Hacking Your Mortgage Debt to Create Passive Income

"Invest in health, invest in love, invest in knowledge, and above all, invest in compound interest."

Unknown

Paying of your mortgage is a major step towards eliminating debt and increasing your passive income. Paying interest for 30 years can greatly reduce your capacity to save. You need to have a place to live and you need to eventually own your home. For that reason, it's important to plan how you pay off your mortgage in order to free up additional cash that can be saved to produce interest income that compounds monthly.

How do you pay off your mortgage sooner? There are a number of things you can do to pay off your mortgage sooner. How much sooner you pay off your mortgage is entirely up to you and your capacity to reduce expenses and generate more income. Here is a summary of things you can do to pay off your mortgage sooner:

1. Start making bi-weekly payments instead of monthly payments.

2. Eliminate mortgage insurance.

3. Get a 15 year mortgage instead of 30 years, if you can afford the payments.

4. Reduce other expenses in order to increase how much you can pay towards principal every month.

5. Shop around for insurance and get all the possible discounts to have more cash available to pay down your mortgage.

6. Improve your credit score so that you can get the lowest interest rates.

7. Apply for property tax exemptions that you may qualify for and pay early to get additional discounts. This will free up more cash to pay down your mortgage.

8. Rent space in your house for additional income and use this additional income to pay down your mortgage. Ex.: Guest house, extra room, etc.

Doing all these things should allow you to pay off your mortgage faster than you ever thought possible.

If we use some general numbers you will see the effect these 8 things can have on your ability to eliminate your mortgage. If you create a mortgage plan similar to this you will free up cash and you will no longer have to make mortgage payments. You will still have to pay insurance and taxes on your home but these are not considered interest payments which is what we are trying to get rid of so that we can start getting paid interest every month instead.

ACCELERATED MORTGAGE PAY OFF EXAMPLE

Current financial situation:

30 year mortgage Loan amount: $200,000

Interest rate: 5%

Mortgage insurance: $175

Mortgage payment: $1,074

Insurance payments: $150 per month

Property taxes: $200 per month

Other expenses: $2,600

Current income: $6,000

Rental income: $0

Savings capacity each month: $1,801

NOTE: These numbers are not meant to be precise figures and are just used for example purposes as interest rates can fluctuate and what you actually qualify for may be different.

To calculate how much we have available to save each month we need to subtract your total income from your total expenses.

Total income - Total expenses = Savings capacity

$6,000 - $4,199 = $1,801

Amount you can save each month: $1,801

If you followed the 8 step process provided, you could have a situation that looks more like this:

Improved financial situation:

15 year mortgage Loan amount: $200,000

Interest rate: 5%

Mortgage insurance: $0

Mortgage payment: $1,582

Insurance payments: $90

Property taxes: $120

Other expenses: $1,500

Current income: $6,000

Rental income: $500

Amount you can save each month: $3,208

$6,500 – $3,292 = $3,208

Final financial situation:

When you finish pay off your mortgage your total savings capacity should be $4,790.

$3,208 + $1,582 = $4,790

Amount you save every month plus old mortgage payment you can now save will result in $4,790.

We went from having $1,081 in savings every month to having $4,790 you are capable of saving each month once you pay off your mortgage.

What these three examples show us:

Current financial situation: By saving $1,801 per month for 30 years at a 1% interest rate that compounds monthly, you should have a total of $755,750.

This is how your interest will compound over 30 years:

Year 1: $21,711

Year 2: $43,641

Year 3: $65,791

Year 4: $88,163

Year 5: $110,760

Year 6: $133,584

Year 7: $156,637

Year 8: $179,922

Year 9: $203,441

Year 10: $227,196

Year 11: $251,190

Year 12: $275,424

Year 30: $755,750

We skipped years 13 – 29 to simplify the example but the key is to notice the gradual growth when using compound interest.

Improved financial situation: By saving $3,208 per month for 30 years at a 1% interest rate that compounds monthly, you should have a total of $1,346,167.

This is how your interest will compound over 30 years:

Year 1: $38,673

Year 2: $77,734

Year 3: $117,188

Year 4: $157,038

Year 5: $197,289

Year 6: $237,944

Year 7: $279,007

Year 8: $320,483

Year 9: $362,375

Year 10: $404,689

Year 11: $447,427

Year 12: $490,595

Year 30: $1,346,167

We skipped years 13 – 29 to simplify the example but the key is to notice the gradual growth when using compound interest.

Final financial situation: By saving $4,790 per month for 30 years at a 1% interest rate that compounds monthly, you should have a total of $2,010,019.

This is how your interest will compound over 30 years:

Year 1: $57,744

Year 2: $116,068

Year 3: $174,979

Year 4: $234,481

Year 5: $294,580

Year 6: $355,284

Year 7: $416,597

Year 8: $478,527

Year 9: $541,078

Year 10: $604,258

Year 11: $668,072

Year 12: $732,528

Year 30: $2,010,019

We skipped years 13 – 29 to simplify the example but the key is to notice the gradual growth when using compound interest.

CHAPTER SUMMARY

The largest form of interest payments you will make in your life will be on your mortgage. This is a big opportunity to go from owing to owning. Finding a way to pay it off and eliminate having to pay interest should be on the top of your list. Once you have paid off your mortgage and have no interest payments, you can use the interest savings to increase your interest income every month by earning interest on interest (compound interest). Pay yourself the same amount you were paying your mortgage on a monthly basis, but do it so that you earn interest on it by depositing it into an interest earning savings account that compounds interest on a monthly basis.

Chapter 5

How to Switch Car Payments for Interest Payments

"He who understands it, earns it ... he who doesn't ... pays it."

Albert Einstein

Having car payments for most people is a common thing. This a normal expense that people have to incur on a monthly basis. The goal is not to have any payments at all if you have the option to pay it cash, even if it means downgrading to an older model or a different model all together so that you can eventually pay it off within a year or two or less. If your current car payments are $400 per month, and assuming you finish paying it off so that you don't have car payments any more, you would essentially have $400 available to save and start earning interest on. How would this change affect your finances over the long term? How would the same $400 grow over 30 years if the interest is compounded monthly?

Let's see how much the same $400 would grow over 30 years when you deposit them into an interest earning savings account that compounds interest on a monthly basis with an interest rate of 1%.

This is how interest will compound over 30 years when depositing $400 every month instead making a car payment:

Year 1: $4,822

Year 2: $9,693

Year 3: $14,612

Year 4: $19,581

Year 5: $24,600

Year 6: $29,669

Year 7: $34,789

Year 8: $39,690

Year 9: $45,184

Year 10: $50,460

Year 11: $55,789

Year 12: $61,171

Year 30: $167,851

We skipped years 13 – 29 to simplify the example but the key is to notice the gradual growth when using compound interest.

After 30 years of making $400 deposits into your savings account every month you would have a total of $167,851.

In this case, you replaced your car payments with monthly savings account deposits and can now see how this can have an incredible effect over your ability to save. This is the reason why it's so important to lower and even eliminate as many expenses as possible. Car payments are another expense that you should figure out a way to lower or eliminate.

Let's look at some examples so we can compare how much you can save with different car payment amounts:

If you make $300 in car payments every month, you could replace car payments for interest payments by paying off your car, and accumulate a total of $125,888 over 30 years in an interest earning savings account that compounds interest on a monthly basis and has a 1% interest rate.

This is how interest will compound over 30 years when depositing $300 every month instead making a car payment:

Year 1: $3,617

Year 2: $7,269

Year 3: $10,959

Year 4: $14,686

Year 5: $18,450

Year 6: $22,252

Year 7: $26,092

Year 8: $29,970

Year 9: $33,888

Year 10: $37,845

Year 11: $41,842

Year 12: $45,879

Year 30: $125,888

We skipped years 13 – 29 to simplify the example but the key is to notice the gradual growth when using compound interest.

If you make $500 in car payments every month you could replace car payments for interest payments, by paying off your car, and accumulate a total of $209,814 over 30 years in an interest earning savings account that compounds interest on a monthly basis and has a 1% interest rate.

This is how interest will compound over 30 years when depositing $500 every month instead making a car payment:

Year 1: $6,028

Year 2: $12,116

Year 3: $18,265

Year 4: $24,476

Year 5: $30,750

Year 6: $37,086

Year 7: $43,486

Year 8: $49,951

Year 9: $56,480

Year 10: $63,075

Year 11: $69,736

Year 12: $76,484

Year 30: $209,814

We skipped years 13 – 29 to simplify the example but the key is to notice the gradual growth when using compound interest.

If you make $700 in car payments every month you could replace car payments for interest payments, by paying off your car, and accumulate a total of $293,740 over 30 years in an interest earning savings account that compounds interest on a monthly basis and has a 1% interest rate.

This is how interest will compound over 30 years when depositing $700 every month instead making a car payment:

Year 1: $8,439

Year 2: $16,962

Year 3: $25,571

Year 4: $34,266

Year 5: $43,049

Year 6: $51,920

Year 7: $60,881

Year 8: $69,931

Year 9: $79,072

Year 10: $88,305

Year 11: $97,631

Year 12: $107,050

Year 30: $293,740

We skipped years 13 – 29 to simplify the example but the key is to notice the gradual growth when using compound interest.

CHAPTER SUMMARY

Paying interest on a depreciating asset is a bad financial decision. First of all, you are paying interest which is what you're trying to stay away from. Second, you're paying interest on an asset (your car) that goes down in value as time goes by. Always find a way to minimize depreciation by buying almost new cars (minimally used but in great condition) so that you save yourself the biggest drop in value which usually happens when you buy a brand new car. Also, figure out a way to pay off your car soon so that you are not paying interest on it. Once it's paid off, take the original car payments you were making and start depositing them into an interest earning savings account so that you can start earning interest on interest.

Chapter 6

Hacking your savings account

"The drafts which true genius draws upon posterity, although they may not always be honored so soon as they are due, are sure to be paid with compound interest in the end."

Charles Caleb Colton

Compound interest is easy to create and fast to accumulate once you start. Open an interest earning savings account at a bank (make sure to find a bank that offers the highest paying interest rate). Start making deposits every month in a specific amount that you can afford to make. Remember, the more you deposit, the more interest you will accumulate. It's amazing how even a low interest rate can allow you to accumulate interest income fast.

Savings accounts at different banks can compound monthly, quarterly, or annually. Always search for the shortest time frame which is commonly the monthly option. Make sure you are getting paid monthly interest on your savings. Many online banks offer higher interest rates than banks with physical branches since they don't have the overhead costs of maintaining those branches. You should research to see what some online banks are paying in interest. Make sure you don't get an account that has maintenance charges or minimum balance fees as these expenses will eat up your interest payments. Some banks even pay you a bonus when you open an account with a specific amount which is a great way to start saving as long as there are no hidden fees or requirements every month.

When you start making monthly deposits to your savings account try to be consistent with the amount you put in and make sure it's done on a specific day each month so that you can start making it a habit. Having automatic transfers made on a specific day each month to be withdrawn from your checking account to your savings account is a great idea.

Make sure the transfer happens within one or two days after you receive your salary payment so that you don't spend the money before you transfer it. Many successful investors suggest that you save at least 10% of what you make each month and always pay yourself first before paying all your other expenses. This is a better way of guaranteeing that you stick with the plan instead of guessing every month how much you should be depositing into your interest earning savings account.

Why are liquid assets a good thing to have?

Remember, savings accounts are liquid assets which means you can withdraw your money at any moment. If you find another bank that's offering a higher interest rate, you can take your money to that bank the very same day. Having liquid assets gives you flexibility as to what options you have for its use. If you have a certificate of deposit, you will accrue interest but you cannot withdraw your money until the contract expires or else you will have interest penalties and possibly other fees, plus interest won't automatically compound every month. Also, when you have a CD you are locked to that interest rate and won't benefit at all if banks start paying a higher interest rate on their savings or money market accounts during that time period. That's why it's important to consider a high interest rate as well as having the flexibility to move your money when you want.

Benefits of having a savings account:

- It can compound interest on a monthly basis.
- It's liquid and available to you any time.
- Some interest rates can be as high as other money market accounts or CD's.
- You have the flexibility to move your money to another higher paying interest account.
- You can normally make as many deposits as you want.

- It's considered a safer investment than other non-FDIC insured products.

Negative aspects of having a savings account:

- You could be receiving a higher interest rate on another investment.
- It will only grow if you continue to make additional deposits and/or continue to be paid interest on it.
- You won't have the benefit of dividend payments or equity as you would in other investments.

COMPOUND INTEREST EXAMPLES

Considering that everyone has a different financial situation when it comes to saving, I will provide different savings amounts and interest rates showing how compound interest could benefit you over 30 years.

Assuming the interest is compounded monthly.

If you make monthly deposits of $500 into a savings account earning 1%

If you have a savings account earning 1% (on average over 30 years) and you deposit the same amount every month which in this case would be $500, you would accumulate approximately $209,814.

If you make monthly deposits of $500 into a savings account earning 2%

If you have a savings account earning 2% (on average over 30 years) and you deposit the same amount every month which in this case would be $500, you would accumulate approximately $246,363.

If you make monthly deposits of $500 into a savings account earning 3%

If you have a savings account earning 3% (on average over 30 years) and you deposit the same amount every month

which in this case would be $500, you would accumulate approximately $291,368.

If you make monthly deposits of $1,000 into a savings account earning 1%

If you have a savings account earning 1% (on average over 30 years) and you deposit the same amount every month which in this case would be $1,000, you would accumulate approximately $419,628.

If you make monthly deposits of $1,000 into a savings account earning 2%

If you have a savings account earning 2% (on average over 30 years) and you deposit the same amount every month which in this case would be $1,000, you would accumulate approximately $492,725.

If you make monthly deposits of $1,000 into a savings account earning 3%

If you have a savings account earning 3% (on average over 30 years) and you deposit the same amount every month which in this case would be $1,000, you would accumulate approximately $582,737.

If you make monthly deposits of $2,000 into a savings account earning 1%

If you have a savings account earning 1% (on average over 30 years) and you deposit the same amount every month which in this case would be $2,000, you would accumulate approximately $839,256.

If you make monthly deposits of $2,000 into a savings account earning 2%

If you have a savings account earning 2% (on average over 30 years) and you deposit the same amount every month which in this case would be $2,000, you would accumulate approximately $985,451.

If you make monthly deposits of $2,000 into a savings account earning 3%

If you have a savings account earning 3% (on average over 30 years) and you deposit the same amount every month which in this case would be $2,000, you would accumulate approximately $1,165,474.

If you make monthly deposits of $4,000 into a savings account earning 1%

If you have a savings account earning 1% (on average over 30 years) and you deposit the same amount every month

which in this case would be $4,000, you would accumulate approximately $1,678,513.

If you make monthly deposits of $4,000 into a savings account earning 2%

If you have a savings account earning 2% (on average over 30 years) and you deposit the same amount every month which in this case would be $4,000, you would accumulate approximately $1,970,902.

If you make monthly deposits of $4,000 into a savings account earning 3%

If you have a savings account earning 3% (on average over 30 years) and you deposit the same amount every month which in this case would be $4,000, you would accumulate approximately $2,330,948.

If you make monthly deposits of $6,000 into a savings account earning 1%

If you have a savings account earning 1% (on average over 30 years) and you deposit the same amount every month which in this case would be $6,000, you would accumulate approximately $2,517,769.

If you make monthly deposits of $6,000 into a savings account earning 2%

If you have a savings account earning 2% (on average over 30 years) and you deposit the same amount every month which in this case would be $6,000, you would accumulate approximately $2,956,352.

If you make monthly deposits of $6,000 into a savings account earning 3%

If you have a savings account earning 3% (on average over 30 years) and you deposit the same amount every month which in this case would be $6,000, you would accumulate approximately $3,496,421.

If you make monthly deposits of $8,000 into a savings account earning 1%

If you have a savings account earning 1% (on average over 30 years) and you deposit the same amount every month which in this case would be $8,000, you would accumulate approximately $3,357,026.

If you make monthly deposits of $8,000 into a savings account earning 2%

If you have a savings account earning 2% (on average over 30 years) and you deposit the same amount every month

which in this case would be $8,000, you would accumulate approximately $3,941,803.

If you make monthly deposits of $8,000 into a savings account earning 3%

If you have a savings account earning 3% (on average over 30 years) and you deposit the same amount every month which in this case would be $8,000, you would accumulate approximately $4,661,895.

If you make monthly deposits of $10,000 into a savings account earning 1%

If you have a savings account earning 1% (on average over 30 years) and you deposit the same amount every month which in this case would be $10,000, you would accumulate approximately $4,196,282.

If you make monthly deposits of $10,000 into a savings account earning 2%

If you have a savings account earning 2% (on average over 30 years) and you deposit the same amount every month which in this case would be $10,000, you would accumulate approximately $4,927,254.

If you make monthly deposits of $10,000 into a savings account earning 3%

If you have a savings account earning 3% (on average over 30 years) and you deposit the same amount every month which in this case would be $10,000, you would accumulate approximately $5,827,369.

What can you see?

You can see from all of these examples, how powerful and effective compound interest is. The more you save, the more interest you can compound over time. That's why it's so important to find a way to reduce expenses and increase your income. This will allow you to save more which will allow you to earn more interest every month.

You don't have to be a math genius to see that small amounts can add up quickly when you make consistent monthly deposits that compound interest on interest. Go and make it happen!

CHAPTER SUMMARY

Compound interest is a hard worker that can be part of your financial life. Make money your employee not your boss by opening an interest earning savings account and make deposits every month on a consistent basis. Check with your bank representative to make sure the interest will compound on a monthly basis so that you can see the effects of compound interest at work.

Remember, you own your money. You're money does not own you. Start making it work hard to so that it grows faster through compound interest.

Chapter 7

Hacking your expenses to create passive income

"Good and evil both increase at compound interest. That is why the little decisions you and I make every day are of such infinite importance."

C. S. Lewis

Most people get into the habit of paying for things they don't really need and don't even use. Subscriptions and annual credit card payments are commonly paid for and unnecessary in most cases. Making a detailed list of what you pay for every month will provide you with a glimpse of what you're spending on and where you could be saving. Create an expenses eliminating plan to help you make it happen.

Here is a list of expenses that you could have and would benefit by eliminating or lowering them.

- Eating out
- Annual credit card fees
- Email or website subscriptions
- Plastic water bottles
- Junk food

- Non-discounted apparel
- Cable TV
- Internet
- Gasoline
- Car insurance
- School supplies.
- Medical bills
- Shopping sprees.
- Travel
- Business expenses
- Water bill
- Electrical bill
- Rent or mortgage
- Car payments
- Income taxes
- Cell phone

These are just a few of the expenses most people have but you can always add more to the list.

Let's go over them one by one:

Eating out can be a lot of fun but often expensive and not very healthy. Try preparing food at home and taking it to work. You will find you lose weight faster when you bring your own food to work than eating out. Going on a picnic or eating outdoors can also be relaxing and good for you when you eat healthy and nourishing foods. Most restaurants that are available during lunch and dinner offer foods high in carbs which ultimately make you gain weight in an unhealthy manner. They often offer some form of bread product such as: pizza, subs, sandwiches, pasta, wraps, etc. Lean proteins, fruits, salads, and nuts are known to help control body weight and provide you with less ups and downs in your energy levels throughout the day.

Annual credit card fees are often unnecessary and take a chunk of your savings out of your pocket for no reason at all. Call your credit card company and ask them if you can downgrade your credit card or eliminate the annual fee they charge. Most of the time they will help you resolve this. Don't give away money for free.

Email or website subscriptions can be forgotten expenses that appear every month or on an annual basis and go unnoticed. I am sure they were important at one point or another but are they necessary now? Go over all your subscriptions and see what you really use and what you don't need any more. You will be surprised to find out what you're paying for and not using at all any more.

Plastic Water bottles should be used only in emergency situations and not as an everyday thing. Find a water container that you can comfortably carry with you and fill it with water. If you want high quality water, simply purchase a water filter system that will reduce the toxins in your drinking water. For the best quality water, buy a reverse osmosis water filter. These are not as expensive as most people think and often provide a significant benefit when it comes to the quality of water you drink. These can eliminate a large portion of toxins and other materials found in water including: metals, chlorine, fluoride, bacteria, etc. Some water bottles sold in stores don't provide the quality they advertise. If you want to check the quality of the water in your bottle, simply use a mini water quality tester. They are very inexpensive and worth the money. When you check the quality of the water your drinking using one of these water quality testers, you won't like what you see and will feel compelled to buy a reverse osmosis water filtration system. These are one-time expenses instead of recurring expenses as would be the case when you purchase water bottles on a daily or weekly basis.

Junk food tastes good but can add up both in expenses and on your belly. If you make it a habit of carrying healthy foods with you instead of eating what's available to you when you go out, you will find it much easier to resist the temptation. Become a food carrier. Take a pouch, small back pack, purse, and fill it with raw fruit, dry fruit, nuts, vegetables, and other healthy and delicious foods. It's very simple, all you need to do is plan ahead what you want to eat the next day and put it in your carrying case for the next day or for the remainder of the day. Most junk foods have no nutritional value which means your body gets nothing from eating it. No vitamins, no minerals, no energy, no positive benefits. The effects of healthy food versus junk food, will compound over time. If your stomach is full of healthy food, you won't be interested in junk food. If you're at the supermarket, simply skip the isles that carry junk food and make it a habit of not going through them anymore.

Non-discounted apparel is an easy expense to reduce. Simply plan ahead. Find out what you want and when it will be on sale. Some stores have annual sales on specific dates or seasons. Remember to buy your winter clothing in the summer and summer clothing in the winter as they will have the biggest discounts during these times of the year. Making purchases online is also a great way to save. Online retail stores often offer a discounted price that you won't get if you purchase the same article by going to a physical store.

Cable TV has been a favorite expense for most households for many years but times have changed and new technology has allowed many people to eliminate cable and replace it with online apps that you can access through your phone that can project on your TV. There are devices that allow you to stream your favorite shows and movies on to your TV from your smart phone that don't require a monthly subscription. They become a one-time expense.

Internet is necessary for most people and an expense they must have in order to conduct business and other daily activities. For this reason, it's a good idea to shop around for the best internet service rates in your market. Most internet providers have a special going on that they won't mention if you don't ask so make sure to call and ask.

Gasoline has been a classic expense for all those who own a car. Thanks to hybrid, electric, and soon to be solar powered cars, the cost of gas will be greatly reduced. Consider these options when buying a car as they will save you a significant amount of money over time. If you don't have any of these types of cars and still want to save on gas, shop around town for the lowest gas prices and go there from now on. Other ways to save are: getting a discount gas card, downgrading to a smaller vehicle, lowering your air conditioning consumption, getting new tires, etc.

Car insurance is a very inconsistent expense when it comes to car insurance providers. If you call one insurance company versus another, there can be an almost double or triple the cost difference. Always shop around for the lowest insurance prices since this can save you money. Make sure to ask them what discounts they can provide you with since you might not be receiving a discount they offer and you qualify for. Make more than two calls and make sure you call the largest companies as they can offer the lowest rates most of the time.

School supplies can be expensive or inexpensive depending on what you need and the cost of those things. If you or your kids have to pay for school supplies always shop online first as you will often find lower prices than going to the store. If you want to go to the store instead of buying online, make sure you find the same article online and print the item with the price on it so that you can have the store price-match what is advertised online. Many physical stores have adopted this option to be able to compete against online stores. Another great way to save on school supplies is to buy what you need months in advance as most prices go up right before school starts which means you paid more than you should have. If you know you will have the same expenses the following year, purchase those things in advance when they are on sale which is usually when school has already started and people stop buying school supplies. Stores need to get rid of inventory so they sell the same school supplies at much lower prices.

Medical bills can be a difficult expense to cover. Make sure you plan ahead by having health insurance and shopping around before you pay for medicine, check-ups, shots and other medical expenses that would not be considered an emergency. One pharmacy might be charging 30-40% more than their competitor which could be located right across the street.

Shopping sprees can be avoided if you know what you're looking to purchase in advance. Make a list of all the things you want to buy before leaving your home. That way, you will have a shopping plan you are prepared to follow. Next, stick to the list. Don't plan on buying 10 things and leave with 20. Also, know the difference between needing and wanting something. If you don't need it and won't use it more than once, think again.

Travel is a fun and exciting expense everyone has about once a year even if you just drive to another city and don't necessarily take a plane or train. Book trips online and in advance to get the best deals. Be flexible if you can on dates and on the location as many places around the world are in low demand on different times of the year which can reduce your overall expenses and provide you with some unique experiences. Using airline miles, travel points, and car rental coupons are other ways you can get significant discounts or simply reduce your total travel expenses.

Business expenses are important and many times necessary. Decide what expenses have the most significant benefit on your company or home and which don't. Some expenses are large but don't provide you with a significant benefit. Analyze all your business expenses in detail as you will always find something you don't need and can eliminate.

Your **water bill** is an expense you can have control over by doing a number of different things. You can close the water faucet while you brush your teeth or shave. You can learn to rinse the dishes and then close the water faucet when you are cleaning them. Take shorter showers and prevent leaving the water running for too long before you get into the shower. There are many more things you can do to lower your water bill, be creative and don't let water run if you're not using it.

Your **electrical bill** can be easily reduced by doing some very simple things. Turn off lights when you leave the house or when you're not in a particular room. Turn off the TV if you're not watching it. Wash your clothes when you can fill up the washer instead of washing every time you have a few things. Lower your air conditioning or heater consumption but using it when you need it instead of just leaving it on.

Rent and mortgage expenses are usually large expenses. The general rule is that it's better to own than to rent if you can afford it and if it allows you to save after covering all expenses. Then, it's always better to own your home free and clear instead of having a mortgage so you need to work on paying off your mortgage in an intelligent manner. I have covered an entire chapter on this topic so you can review it and see if you can benefit from some of the ideas provided. This is an important expense you need to go over and find a way to reduce.

Car payments have increased over the years. Before, making $500 car payments was high but now $1,200 is considered a high payment. For this reason, it makes sense to reduce or eliminate this expense by using a number of different options such as: paying your car off, downgrading to a slightly older model but still in great condition, getting a lower priced vehicle, getting an older vehicle that won't require payments at all, etc. There are many different options you can choose from. Your objective is to lower or eliminate your car payments.

Tax payments are important for society as a whole but may not be an expense you need to have. Owning a business and taking advantage of the way expenses are allowed to be deducted first before tax payments, should be something you should consider. It would be wise for you to talk to your accountant to see if you could benefit from this option.

Lower your **cell phone** bill. Call your phone provider and find a plan that allows you to reduce your payments. See if you are paying for internet you're not using every month or have services you have never used that could be eliminated. Pay off your cell phone if you are financing it to lower your monthly payments if necessary. Don't pay high cell phone bills when you could be paying much less. Compare service providers to see if another company offers a different type of plan that would benefit you and save you money.

The Resulting Benefit

By hacking these expenses you can free up cash you can save to start generating interest income from interest payments. Small savings in each of these categories will add up to large amounts. Find a way to reduce these and other expenses in your life.

Let's say you have $2,500 in monthly expenses and are able to reduce them down to $1,000, you would be able to save $1,500 per month. If you were able to save $1,500 every month by depositing these funds into an interest earning savings account paying 1% interest and had this interest compound monthly, you would have a total of $629,442 saved after 30 years. This would be a nice amount of money to retire on and all you had to do was review all your expenses and eliminate or lower them.

CHAPTER SUMMARY

Your household and business expenses are a hidden opportunity to convert outgoing expense payments into incoming passive interest payments. By reducing or eliminating expenses you currently have, you can increase your capacity to save money and start earning interest income. You accumulate so many things and become attached to other things you don't really need. Eliminate the physical and mental clutter in your life. Turn it into passive income. Find a way to release yourself from everyday expenses that will add up in the end to wasted money instead of compounded money.

Chapter 8

Reversing your financial life

"The longer the payment is withholden; the better for you; for compound interest on compound interest is the rate and usage of this exchequer."

Ralph Waldo Emerson

Would you rather receive interest every month or pay interest every month?

This is a simple question that most people answer correctly but in reality do the exact opposite. The large majority of the population pays interest to a bank or lender in one form or another every month. Since everyone is so focused on increasing their income and are busy working harder, they don't realize what's going on. The interest every month simply keeps increasing so they work longer hours and spend less time with loved ones or enjoying life which is not the way it's supposed to be. Take the time to go over your life and how it's projecting towards the future. Are you working more or are you working less and enjoying more free time?

Why not do the opposite?

What if you paid off all your debts and stopped paying interest to others and started to save money? What if the money you saved every month paid you interest? What if the interest compounded every month so you would get paid interest on that interest? These are the questions you need to start asking yourself. These are the questions you need to start answering and doing something about it. The sooner you go from paying interest to receiving interest payments, the faster your income and savings will increase.

What if all the interest you pay in the form of financing became your income? How much would you be making every month? Stop and think about this. Do the numbers and see just how much you could receive in passive interest income per month from simply having the courage to be different than the rest and eliminating your debts.

The smartest and wealthiest people in the world follow this rule. They work hard to stay out of debt and not have to pay interest. They also use the power of compound interest to increase their net worth and their quality of life.

What's your financial situation?

Let's say this is your situation every month:

Net income: $7,000

Interest payments on debt you owe: $680

Other expenses: $4,300

Savings account (assets): 30,000

Total monthly savings: 2,020

Let's see how much you could accumulate over 30 years using compound interest with an interest rate of 1% compounded monthly.

At the end of 30 years you would have compounded a total of $888,140 when you use your $30,000 in savings as your initial account opening deposit to start accumulating compound interest.

TOTAL COMPOUNDED INTEREST: $888,140

If you pay off all your debts

What if you paid off all your debts and eliminated your interest payments by using $25,000 of your savings?

Let's see what this would look like every month:

Net income: $7,000

Other expenses: $4,300

Savings account (assets): 5,000

Total monthly savings: $2,700

At the end of 30 years you would have compounded a total of $1,139,745 when you use your $5,000 as your initial account opening deposit to start accumulating compound interest.

TOTAL COMPOUNDED INTEREST: $1,139,745

If you pay your debts off and eliminate expenses

What if you paid off all your debts and eliminated your interest payments by using $25,000 of your savings assets, and lowered your expenses down to $2,000 every month?

Let's see what this would look like every month:

Net income: $7,000

Other expenses: $2,000

Savings account (assets): 5,000

Total monthly savings: $5,000

At the end of 30 years you would have compounded a total of $2,104,890 when you use your $5,000 as your initial account opening deposit to start accumulating compound interest.

TOTAL COMPOUNDED INTEREST: $2,104,890

What's the difference?

The difference between paying interest and having high expenses or eliminating all debt and lowering your expenses was that your savings capacity grew from $2,020 to $5,000 every month.

When you look at what you were able to save using compound interest initially ($888,140) to what you were able to save after eliminating all your debts and lowering your expenses ($2,104,890), you have a difference of $1,216,750. This is a big difference when it comes to saving.

$2,104,890 - $888,140 = $1,216,750

You were able to save an additional $1,216,750 over 30 years simply by paying off your debts and lowering your expenses.

That's why it's a good idea to eliminate interest payments and lower your expenses.

CHAPTER SUMMARY

For people who think that paying off their debts won't change their finances, think again. By paying off your debts, everything will change. It will allow you to save more and increase the amount of money you can compound every month. By eliminating expenses, you created an even greater ripple effect over time. Make it your priority to increase your saving capacity. In order to save more you need to spend less and make more money. Both of which are entirely up to you. Stop paying others and start paying yourself interest. Learn to live a financially free life and end financially slavery.

Chapter 9:

Becoming a Compound Interest Millionaire

"Nature uses compounding effects to grow and spread. Humans should use compound interest to grow and spread financially."

Unknown

Becoming a compound interest millionaire is very possible. To become a compound interest millionaire you can start by doing the following simple but effective things:

1. Add up all of your debt and find out how long it would take you to pay it off.
2. Pay off all your debts one by one no matter how large they may seem.
3. Decide what sacrifices you need to make in your life to reduce expenses and increase savings.
4. Increase your income by being creative: getting another job, starting your own business, baby-sitting, tutoring, cutting the lawn for neighbors, renting space (guest house, rooms, other space.) in your home, etc.
5. Add all the payments you eliminated and deposit them into your interest earning savings account from now on.

6. Use a compound interest calculator and figure out how long it would take you to become a millionaire just using the deposits you would make from the payments you eliminated and the resulting income you are able to save every month. For example, if you're expenses are $2,200 per month and you found a way to cut expenses and pay off all your debts so that this amount would become $1,000 now, you would deposit the amount off payments you eliminated every month into an interest earning savings account, along with the income you have left over ($1,200 expenses + $3,000 in income = $4,200 to be deposited). Use an initial interest rate of 1% even though the 30 year average interest rate on your savings account might be higher in the end. Make sure you choose the option to compound interest monthly since you should be receiving interest payments monthly not annually.

7. Once you calculate how long it would take you to become a millionaire using the deposits from the eliminated expenses plus whatever income is left over after paying the resulting expenses, you can play around with different increases or decreases in your income so that you are prepared for changes in your financial future and can prepare for them in advance.

8. On the compound interest calculator use 2% as the interest rate and then 3% to see how long it would take you to reach a million as well in case you are consistently able to find a higher paying savings account. Don't go higher

than 3% because you need to use a number that will be realistic when averaging interest rates over 30 years. Savings account interest rates will go up and down every year so use a low number for calculation purposes. Make sure you shop around to find the bank that pays the most interest, even if it's an online bank.

9. When you figure out how long it will take you to reach a million, reduce this time by increasing the amount you need to save every month.

10. If you want to accelerate the process, find a way to increase your income and reduce your expenses even more. Start a business, switch to a higher paying job, ask for a raise, lower your taxes with the help of your accountant, etc.

What's next?

Take control of your financial life and your future. Stop depending on others to give you solutions by providing high risk investments or unrealistic future outcomes for your money. Take charge and allow yourself to have the freedom to enjoy your life the way you want to. Having to stress over finances should be unnecessary if you plan ahead and prepare to be successful.

Wealthy people don't pay interest. Wealthy people live off interest payments and passive income. They use businesses to take advantage of tax benefits to maximize their earning potential and save even more. Start using compound interest in your finances and in your life. Begin by compounding love, compounding health, compounding your capacity to share and care for others, compounding your relationships, and compounding your life in general.

CHAPTER SUMMARY

Follow the steps outlined in this chapter. Prevent yourself from deviating from the plan and stick with your savings goal. Be disciplined with your expenses. When you start to see the positive financial results, you will feel energized and motivated to continue forward with what you're doing. It will compound emotionally in your life. You will be happier, more energetic, and more motivated to increase your earning capacity and save more. Doing this will change your life.

Chapter 10

Summing Everything Up

"Pay close attention to the compounding effects in your life for they will be your result in the end."

Unknown

In general, the key component to increasing your compound interest is to increase the amount you're able to save each month. In order to do this you want to do three very important things:

#1 Lower all your expenses and eliminate debts

Go over all your expenses and see which ones are not necessary or can be eliminated. By lowering your expenses, you will increase your savings capacity.

Here's a simple example:

Total household income: $6,000

Total expenses: $3,000

Savings Capacity per month: $3,000

If you lowered your expenses down to $2,000, your total savings would increase to $4,000 every month.

$6,000 - $2,000 = $4,000 in total savings per month.

#2 Start your own business instead of being an employee

Remember, when you own your business you will be able to deduct expenses before paying taxes which will benefit you and allow you to save more.

Here's an example of what a salaried person saves each month:

Salaried person

Total taxable household income: $6,000

30% taxes: $1,800

Total net household income: $4,200

Total expenses: $2,000

Savings Capacity per month: $2,200

$6,000 x 0.30 = $1,800

$6,000 - $1,800 = $4,200

$4,200 - $2,000 = $2,200 total savings you can start earning interest on.

Here's an example of what a business owner saves each month:

Business owner

Total household income: $6,000

Total expenses: $2,000

Total taxable household income: $4,000

30% taxes: $1,200

Savings Capacity per month: $2,800

$6,000 - $2,000 = $4,000

$4,000 x 0.30 = $1,200

$4,000 - $1,200 = $2,800 total savings you can start earning interest on.

The business owner was able to save $600 more than a salaried employee. Over time this can add up quickly. In a year, this is $7,200 more. In 10 years, this is $72,000 more. You get the idea.

#3 Deposit your savings each month into an interest earning savings account that compounds interest monthly

As a business owner that is able to save $2,800 each month, you can deposit these savings into a savings account that pays a 1% interest rate and compounds interest on a monthly basis.

After 30 years, your savings should grow to $1,174,959.

It's not magic. It's not something unusual to be able to save this amount of money. It simply works. Compound interest combined with consistent saving will grow to amazing amounts over time. This is how you become a compound interest millionaire.

NOTE: Make sure to have an additional emergency savings account and a separate account for expenses which could be your checking account. This way you will resist the urge to take money from your long term savings account. Your emergency savings account can have lower amounts deposited on a monthly basis as you should not have emergencies all the time but you need to be prepared in case something arises.

CHAPTER SUMMARY

Saving is important but doing it efficiently is even more important. To be more efficient you need to eliminate interest payments. You need to lower and eliminate expenses. You need to lower the amount you pay in taxes by owning a business, after consulting with your account to make sure this is right for. You need to work on increasing your income every month and most importantly, you need to start earning compound interest on a monthly basis. You are basically reorganizing your life so that you can have a happier financial future that you can be proud of.

Share the knowledge

How would the world change if less people were in debt and more people had passive income in the form of interest income every month? Would people be less stressed out? Would most people have more free time to spend with family and doing the things they love? How can you help others to achieve real financial freedom and have a truly successful financial future? You can start by sharing this book with them.

The choice to be financially free is really theirs but they need the knowledge. If they knew there was a better way, most people would change their path. Life is all about perspective. How you look at things. If you think becoming financial free is possible, than you are right and if you think the opposite, you are also right. What you decide to do becomes your future so decide to become financially free and help others to do the same.

If you have kids, teach them to become smarter about money at an early age instead of watching them suffer the debt cycle so many people live through. They have to start somewhere, you might as well get them started on the right track by teaching them the importance of saving and being mindful of your expenses. They will follow your lead so set a good example for them.

LEARN – APPLY - SHARE

Vocabulary

Annual percentage yield: is commonly known as the effective annual rate of return when you are taking into account the effect of compound interest.

Annual percentage rate: is the cost of credit expressed as an interest rate which includes all interest and fees.

Annuity: is a financial product that is designed to grow funds received from an individual and eventually pay out a stream of payments to the individual at a later point in time.

Assets: any item owned that increases your net worth. Assets can be tangible or intangible. Assets can be liquid (immediately available, ex: cash.) or illiquid (not immediately available, ex: house.).

Borrower debt cycle: the progression of continued borrowing that eventually leads to the inability to make payments.

Business expenses: are the necessary costs of running a business and can include: utilities, rent, mortgage, water, office supplies, insurance, etc.

Business profits: is the amount of revenue or financial benefit left over after all expenses, costs, and taxes in a business.

Compound interest: is the interest calculated on the original principal and on the accumulated interest of past periods. Also known as "interest on interest".

Compound interest calculator: a calculator that shows you how compound interest can increase your savings over time.

Certificate of deposit: is a savings certificate with a fixed maturity date that pays a fixed interest on the principal deposited. The interest is paid at the maturity date.

Checking account: is a bank account that offers easy access to your money. Checking accounts allow you to write checks, withdraw funds, deposit funds, make purchases, pay bills, and is considered a liquid asset.

Debt: money that is owed or due that must be paid back at a later time.

Depreciation: the loss in value of an asset over its useful life.

Employee: someone who is hired for salaries or wages by an employer to do a specific job or task.

Home equity: the value of ownership in a house that is represented by the current market value minus all loan balances. It's the homeowner's interest in a home.

Household expenses: a breakdown of personal living expenses such as: rent, mortgage, utilities, food, lawn care, repairs, etc.

Interest income: is income that is derived in the form of interest earned in a bank deposit over time.

Money market account: is a type of bank savings account that earns a higher interest over time than a regular savings account. It often has a minimum deposit amount and other restrictions as to withdrawals and deposits.

Net Worth: is the value of everything you currently own minus all of your debts. Assets minus liabilities equals net worth.

Passive income: is income that is received in the form of cash that requires little or no effort to maintain it.

Real estate rental income: is income that is derived from renting a dwelling unit minus all expenses to maintain it.

Rental income: is any income you receive for the use of property.

Savings: money that has been accumulated and set aside.

Savings account: is a bank account that allows you to store up cash securely and often earn interest on that money.

Stock cash dividends: is a form of payment that is made in the form of cash paid out by a company to its investors for the ownership of shares.

www.ingramcontent.com/pod-product-compliance
Lightning Source LLC
Chambersburg PA
CBHW021115210326
41598CB00017B/1451